T

*Addressing Common Sins
and Growing in Faith*

by Sarah Geringer

Copyright © 2017 Sarah Geringer

*To all those wanting to bear
more fruit
for God's glory*

Acknowledgments

First, thanks to my husband and children for your patience, support, and understanding as I pursue my writing dreams.

A big thank you goes out to my launch team members. This book would not be a success without your dedicated help!

Thank you, members of the Heartland Writers Guild. Your constant support lifts me up when I feel like quitting.

Thanks to Michael Hyatt, Jeff Goins, Tim Grahl, Chandler Bolt, and Sarah Mae. Your online training and e-books have powerfully shaped my writing career. I haven't met you yet, but I count you as my mentors.

Above all, thanks go to my Lord and Savior, Jesus Christ, the One who deserves all the glory. I want to bear abundant fruit for your praise alone.

Table of Contents

Welcome to the Fruitful Life   6

Chapter 1: Apathetic or Loving   9

Chapter 2: Irritated or Joyful   17

Chapter 3: Anxious or Peaceful   26

Chapter 4: Impatient or Patient   35

Chapter 5: Selfish or Kind   44

Chapter 6: Worldly or Good   53

Chapter 7: Harsh or Gentle   62

Chapter 8: Scattered or Faithful   70

Chapter 9: Indulgent or Self-Controlled   80

Closing and Bonus Offers   89

About the Author   91

Notes   92

Welcome to the Fruitful Life

But the Holy Spirit produces this kind of fruit in our lives: love, joy, peace, patience, kindness, goodness, faithfulness, gentleness, and self-control. There is no law against these things!

Galatians 5:22-23 NLT

Are you trying hard to live out your faith, yet still struggling with everyday sins like irritation, impatience, and indulgence?

Do you want a mature faith that produces spiritual fruit, no matter what life throws at you?

I've been a Christian for as long as I can remember, but some sins still plague me. Sins like worldliness, lack of commitment, and apathy.

Sometimes I try to justify my sins when I feel convicted. Sometimes I simply ignore the Holy Spirit's promptings to make better choices.

Most often, I feel discouraged because I haven't gotten further along in conquering my sinful nature after so many years in the faith.

I want to be mature, producing spiritual fruit so others may benefit. I don't want to hold my faith all to myself. But my everyday sins, the ones that pester and hang around in bad habits, keep holding me back from the Christ-like person I really want to be.

Everyday sins pile up slowly, like random items in the junk drawer or all kinds of detritus in the hall closet. It's easy to ignore them after a while. It's easier to shut the door or drawer than pull them out and throw them away.

It's easier to feel irritated than loving toward a difficult person.

It's easier to go about my own business than to show kindness to a stranger.

It's easier to speak a harsh word in anger than think first how to give a gentle response.

Yet God wants a fruitful life for us.

This is the life Jesus modeled. He is the Vine, I am the fruit-bearing branch.

This is the life made possible through the Holy Spirit.

I've been going about it all wrong, trying to do it myself. Willing myself to be patient, then a slow driver pulls in front of me, and I complain in front of my children. Forcing myself to be more faithful, then a thousand distractions and the frenetic pace of living pull me away from what's most important.

I wrote this book for me as much as I wrote it for you. In each chapter, we'll look at a common way a fruit of the spirit gets spoiled by sin. We'll reconnect with the Father's original intent for our lives. We'll study how Jesus modeled a fruitful life. We'll ask the Holy Spirit to empower us to overcome these sins, since none of us can do it in our own strength. With this method, we will be set free from the stranglehold of these common sins.

At the end of this book, I want to look back and see how my faith has grown in this process of addressing common sins. I hope you will share how your faith has grown in your process on my blog at sarahgeringer.com.

I've created two special resources to help you bear even more fruit as you read this book. Find out how to gain access to them in the "Closing and Bonus Offers" page near the end of this book.

Are you ready to offer fresh, abundant fruit to God? Let's start cultivating now!

Chapter 1: Apathetic or Loving

Love never gives up, never loses faith, is always hopeful, and endures through every circumstance.
1 Corinthians 13:7

For a long time, I thought hate was love's opposite. Until I experienced apathy, I realized hate is more like love's cousin. Love is passionate, and so is hate. A fire blazes inside whether you kiss or curse.

But when you don't care anymore, no feelings ignite. Apathy feels cold, detached, and dispassionate. Apathy lets the fire die out. Apathy is cool ashes.

What invites apathy, after you once loved or hated? Usually it's self-protection.

Apathy is a cold stone wall, built in the hopes of protecting my heart from getting hurt again.

Right now, I'm in a state of apathy over a difficult relationship. After years of toxicity, this person hurt me so profoundly I can't trust them anymore. I closed my heart to them at the advice of my counselor and several trusted friends.

To be honest, after the climactic conflict I nursed hatred for quite a while. I couldn't believe how someone who professed to be loving and even a believer could be that vicious. For some time, my feelings burned white-hot against my offender.

As years passed, the ashes of that relationship have cooled to the touch. I can run those emotions through my fingers without getting burned anymore. But it's not because I'm happy with how things are now, even though I've forgiven this person. It's because I'm numb from apathy's anesthesia.

Has this happened to you also?

Maybe you disconnect from your marriage because the hurts are too deep.

Maybe you disengage from your extended family because the past is too messy.

Maybe you show up to work to make a dollar, but you don't care about the company anymore because someone took advantage of you.

I've been in all those places before. I know exactly how apathy feels, numb though it may be.

When I endured years of emotional upheaval in my marriage, my heart became apathetic toward the end of our trials. I had given up hope of lasting change. The toxic patterns ingrained in both of us seemed too strong to overcome. Yet God breathed new life into our marriage, and he changed both of our hearts. He opened my heart to giving love and receiving love again. Only with God's help did I learn to love my husband in a healthy way.

When I endured years of suffering in family messes, I was tempted again and again to close myself off in apathy. Deep inside, love stirred and kept me longing for connection. I had to grieve some losses and accept some hard truths while I worked through the problems. In several relationships, I don't feel stuck in apathy any more.

Acceptance is open; apathy is closed. God brought me to the place of acceptance, so I wouldn't slide backward into old, toxic ways of relating. He helped me find healthier ways of showing and accepting love.

In several job situations, I learned my temptation toward apathy was a sign of needing to make a change. While going through trials on the job, I trusted in God's timing, not closing myself off at the first sign of trouble anymore. I stuck tough situations out and became stronger with perseverance. God helped me endure difficult job scenarios because he wanted to grow my faith.

What part of your heart is closed off in apathy?

Do you believe God can show you a new way to love?

I like this quote from Jen Wilkin regarding how God gives new life through the fruits of the spirit:

We cannot create hope where there is hopelessness or love where there is lovelessness. We cannot create repentance where there is unrepentance, but we can cry out to the God who can. In that first great act of creation, God miraculously rendered something from nothing. And he rejoices to continue that work in human hearts. God may restore a broken relationship or circumstance, or he may simply restore hope to you in their midst. Not everything will be made new in this lifetime, but his promise to grow in us the fruit of the Spirit means we can know abundant life whether relationships and circumstances heal or not.[1]

I'm working through my hidden areas of apathy now, opening my heart to God's love so he can help me bear good fruit again.

I want to have an engaged heart rather than a disconnected heart, open to giving and receiving love the way God does.

God's way

To discover how God stays engaged, look no further than the book of Hosea. Hosea had a terribly difficult assignment from God. Listen to what God told Hosea:

"Go and marry a prostitute, so that some of her children will be conceived in prostitution. This will illustrate how Israel has acted like a prostitute by turning against the Lord and worshiping other gods." Hosea 1:2

This woman bore Hosea children, but returned again and again to her sinful life. Hosea had to rescue her out of prostitution, even though chances were high that she would go right back into a sinful lifestyle.

The book of Hosea is a picture of God's undying love for the wayward, stubborn people of Israel. People not so different from you and me. Listen to what God says to his people later in the book:

"I will make you my wife forever, showing you righteousness and justice, unfailing love and compassion." Hosea 2:20

God doesn't close his heart off from you or me, even after we've wounded him time and time again. He stays engaged and keeps pursuing us.

I think it's amazing that the Creator of the universe uses the picture of a jilted husband to portray his commitment to us. He could blast us away in a moment in his omnipotence, yet he always stays engaged. He never becomes numb with apathy. His unfailing love lasts forever.

Jesus' example

During the hours before his trial and crucifixion, Jesus stayed engaged with the disciples, though he knew Judas would betray him and all the others would desert him. He washed their feet, taking the role of the lowest servant, to teach them a powerful lesson about humility. (John 13) He shared his last supper with them, revealing some of his deepest truths (John 14-16). He invited them to keep watch with him while he prayed his deepest prayer (Matthew 26).

Yet just as Jesus predicted, he was betrayed by a kiss of a friend who had followed him for three years. Peter, a member of Jesus' inner circle, denied he even knew Jesus three times. All the other disciples ran away in the moment Jesus needed them most.

Jesus could have withdrawn to a solitary place to spend time alone with God in his last hours, as he often did. However, he chose to spend his last hours before his death with his closest friends, knowing they would hurt him. Jesus chose love instead of hate or apathy.

Holy Spirit's empowerment

God's love never gives up. It never loses faith. It always hopes and endures through every circumstance. His is powerful, transforming love.

I am open to the Holy Spirit working new love in my heart, even in relationships that have turned cold. Reconciliation is a two-way street, and I don't know if my offenders will ever decide to repent. But I am keeping my heart open to the possibility of restored relationships in the future.

I still don't want to be hurt; I want to be wise about how and when to open my heart again. I will rely on the Holy Spirit's prompting. This attitude is far better than apathy.

You and I simply cannot have this kind of love in our own power. We can only receive it from God and then extend it to others. On our own we numb ourselves against getting hurt again. Yet, the Holy Spirit will help us bear the fruit of love in his perfect timing and his perfect wisdom.

As you go through the week ahead, ask the Holy Spirit to help you show love when you feel tempted toward apathy. Remember that you are the branch and Jesus is the Vine; his love will flow through you so you can bear fruit for his glory. God can help you love others the way he would do, if you remain in his love (John 15:1-17).

Prayer:

Heavenly Father, I want to become one who loves, not one who hates or one who doesn't care. Shine your light on my hidden areas of hatred and apathy. Help me face the truth about my sin and recognize my need for your forgiveness. Teach me how to show love when I feel tempted to protect myself against further hurt. Jesus, I am trusting you to serve as my Shepherd, Shield, and Strength. Empower me through your Holy Spirit to bear the fruit of love. In Jesus' name, Amen.

Questions for Study and Reflection:

Read John 15:1-17. What must we do to live a fruitful life, according to this passage?

Love one another

How can you apply John 15:12 in a practical way this week?

By listening, helping, encouraging, and giving someone who needs to hear these words

(To get much more out of this book, go to the "Closing and Bonus Offers" page and gain instant access to the printable Study Guide.)

Chapter 2: Negative or Joyful

How joyful are those who fear the Lord and delight in obeying his commands.
Psalm 112:1

When I'm irritated, I try to quietly relieve the pressure by breathing deeply.

This was working fine for me until I heard how often my husband and children were asking, "Why are you sighing?" when I didn't realize it.

I have more pet peeves than I can count. Maybe my tendency toward perfectionism pushes me toward irritation. Perhaps my tendency toward idealism sets my standards too high. I fall short and so does everyone else. That gap between the ideal and reality triggers my irritation.

And my irritation stems from my natural melancholy bent, the glass-half-empty orientation. My personality is prone to negativity, and I must fight it every day.

When I consider my triggers for irritation, I find a common denominator of frustration when people are inconsiderate of property, time, or feelings.

For example, seeing litter on the roadways pushes my buttons. Watching mile after mile of littered highway makes my heart beat faster, and I'm sure my blood pressure is elevated. *Is it so hard to be responsible for your own trash?* I think. And then my irritation crosses over into judgment, and I feel doubly nasty inside.

I feel irritated when my children dawdle rather than staying focused on getting out the door in the mornings. This pushes my time trigger (though, ironically, I am notorious for arriving late).

I get irritated by pushy salespeople and overly persistent loved ones. Even if people don't intentionally try to annoy me, I tend to take their behaviors personally, and my irritation level soars.

I need to apply this quote from Jerry Bridges in *Respectable Sins*, perhaps while I'm picking up trash from the edges of my woods:

"If you are frequently upset with another person (or persons), you may need to overlook their unintentional actions. Proverbs 19:11, though addressing the topic of anger...says, 'It is [one's] glory to overlook an offense.' And Peter wrote, 'Love covers a multitude of sins' (1 Peter 4:8). We might say that if love covers a multitude of sins, how much more should it cover a multitude of acts that irritate us."[1]

Irritation springs from a negative outlook. Joy springs from a life of faith.

Joy is finding the positive side no matter how negative or irritating the outside situation seems. Joy springs up from a deep well inside, from abiding in the life of the Vine.

I'm writing this book in February, typically the hardest month of the year for me. This is the month winter seems endless. Low grey clouds persist day after day, provoking my seasonal affective disorder. The excitement of the new year is over, and the newness of spring has not yet arrived. February is the month when my irritations spike and my joy is sapped.

This year I've worked hard to fight the temptation of late winter negativity. I began looking for specific instances of joy *within* the doldrums, and I found it in several places:

- The cozy warmth under blankets on a cold night
- Extra family time because we're homebound between the seasons
- Lots of subtly beautiful textures in the quiet winter landscape: grasses, branches, rocks, dry leaves
- Birds returning to sing in the mornings

- Many-colored sunsets more visible in our woods, without leaves blocking the view
- A few late afternoons warm enough for a walk
- The simple joy of meeting with God each morning before anyone else rises

Joy is abundant, if I open my eyes to see it. Joy is a river running underneath every circumstance in the Christian life. It's more powerful than my negativity.

I don't have to wait for life to sail smoothly or become exciting to experience joy. I can find it in any ordinary day, because I am a follower of Christ. This quote by Jerry Bridges inspires me:

Perhaps you don't feel you have too much to show for your life. You haven't written a book, or seen scores come to Christ through your witness, or done anything else that seems significant. But is your name written in heaven? If it is, you have as much reason to rejoice as the most well-known and successful Christian. Nothing you or I will ever do can possibly compare with having our names written in heaven. The most humble Christian as well as the most famous Christian stand together on that common ground.[2]

Now doesn't that give you hope and JOY for today?

I want to be a joy-seeker and a joy-bearer. I want joy to be part of my prayers and vocabulary every single day. I want to be known more for smiling than sighing, even on the coldest, greyest days, because I am full of joy instead of negativity.

God's way

When I think of an irritated person in the Bible, I remember Jonah. He was irritated when God asked him to deliver a message of salvation to a pagan city. He went to great lengths to run away, trapped in negativity. After he obeyed God's command and many thousands of people repented, he still wasn't joyful.

God used a vine to show Jonah his wrongs. The vine grew quickly, shading and soothing Jonah. Then God caused a worm to devour the vine, and Jonah was so irritated he wanted to die! God then spoke to Jonah about his skewed perspective. Jonah had settled into his own opinion, viewing life from his negative outlook rather than through God's eyes. God wanted Jonah to experience the joy of salvation alongside him. He called Jonah to a life of joy, yet the Bible doesn't tell us if Jonah ever accepted the invitation.

God calls you and me to a life of joy also. He wants us to live a righteous life, because it produces the healthy, vigorous growth needed for bearing fruit.

When we fear the Lord and delight in his commands, he gives us joy. Joy carries us through our seasons of sorrow. Joy lifts us up when negativity tries to drag us down. Joy grants us a higher perspective.

Jesus' example

When parents brought their children to Jesus for blessings, the disciples were so irritated they tried to send the families away.

But Jesus said, "Let the children come to me. Don't stop them! For the Kingdom of Heaven belongs to those who are like these children." And he placed his hands on their heads and blessed them before he left. Matthew 19:13-14

The disciples had a negative outlook; they didn't consider children worth Jesus' time. But Jesus wasn't irritated at all. In fact, he told the disciples that a childlike attitude is necessary to get into heaven.

If you want to experience pure joy, spend time with children. They find joy in the smallest things. Their laughter is contagious. They are accepting, open, and teachable. They aren't so jaded as to have a negative outlook (ahem, at least until they become teenagers). No wonder Jesus held children up as examples for a life of abundant faith.

Jesus also promised lasting joy for his followers. The night before his crucifixion, he told his disciples they would have sorrow when he left them. Jesus knew they didn't understand he had to die, and they certainly couldn't comprehend how he would rise from the dead. So, he used the analogy of a woman giving birth to help them understand:

It will be like a woman suffering the pains of labor. When her child is born, her anguish gives way to joy because she has brought a new baby into the world. So you have sorrow now, but I will see you again; then you will rejoice, and no one can rob you of that joy. John 16:21-22

Jesus' resurrection is reason for joy always. This is the cornerstone of our faith. We have the promise of eternal life through Jesus' death and resurrection, and our joy springs from that source. We can always keep that childlike joy in our hearts, once we believe.

Holy Spirit's empowerment

I love this picture of God's people in Jeremiah 17:7-8:
They are like trees planted along a riverbank, with roots that reach deep into the water. Such trees are not bothered by the heat or worried by long months of drought. Their leaves stay green, and they never stop producing fruit.

If we draw our sustenance from God's Word, we will have deep reservoirs of joy to sustain us through every season. We will bear fruit year after year if we remain in Him.

The Holy Spirit will empower you to bear the fruit of joy in positive times and in negative times. You can overcome your negativity and irritation by asking the Holy Spirit to give you joy in His presence.   The joy He grants will overflow into all areas of your fruit bearing.

Heavenly Father, I want to become one who is joyful, not one who is trapped in negativity. Shine your light on my hidden areas of irritation. Help me face the truth about my sin and recognize my need for your correction. Teach me how to show joy when I feel tempted to be negative. Jesus, I am trusting you to serve as my source of positivity and power. Empower me through your Holy Spirit to bear the fruit of joy. In Jesus' name, Amen.

Questions for Study and Reflection:

How does Jonah's negativity remind you of your own? How can you learn from his example?

In what way can you bear joyful fruit for someone else's benefit?

By asking the Holy Spirit to give them Joy in his presence

Chapter 3: Anxious or Peaceful

Make every effort to be found living peaceful lives that are pure and blameless in his sight.
2 Peter 3:14

This year is a milestone: I turn 40, and I also become the mother of a teenager.

These two milestones are known for provoking anxiety for many women. I'm definitely not alone!

The fourth decade threatens my self-worth. *Am I still attractive?* my heart asks silently every time I see a new wrinkle, age spot, grey hair, balding area, or worse—hair where I don't want it. Muscles don't work as well anymore. Weight doesn't fall off with dieting. My internal rhythms are beginning to change, affecting my energy levels.

All these changes are enough to spark worry about my health and appearance every day, if I allow it. Mothering my first teenager could cause all-consuming fear, if I let it begin.

Unknowns swirl: *Will he make good choices? Will he drive safely? Will he hang out with a good crowd or a dangerous crowd?*

Will he be bullied, or will he be a bully? Will he become depressed? Will he start smoking, drinking, or worse? Will he stay pure until marriage? Will he view porn? Will he treat women well? Will he go wild when he moves out?

And the kicker: *Will he keep his faith?*

I can't afford to ask these kinds of questions. I will lose my sanity and drive my son away if I let anxiety have the upper hand. I must make a better choice: the peace that passes all understanding.

I come from a long line of worriers. From a young age I remember learning the language of worry. I heard prudent warnings like "Don't play too close to the road; you'll get run over," and never got within 10 feet of the sidewalk.

 I heard silly directives like "Don't hold your fork like that; you'll never find a husband," and seriously believed I'd become an old maid. My cautious bent predisposed me to worry, and my relatives' good intentions only exacerbated my anxiety.

When I became pregnant with my firstborn, worry threatened to consume me. Any mom can tell you how anxiety arrives the moment pregnancy is known.

These questions swirled: *Will the baby be healthy? Will I be healthy? Will I have a smooth delivery? How dramatically will my schedule change? Will the baby be colicky? How will we afford a new baby and a new house payment at the same time? What kind of parents will we be?*

But God surrounded me with help at just the right time. While I was pregnant, I worked with three other women who had due dates before mine. I watched their bellies grow and listened to their stories, learning so much and gaining hope for my own pregnancy and delivery. I gained peace from a community of people in my same situation.

God is bringing me community in this milestone year. He is introducing me to new friends who have already gone through the 40-year mark. They tell me their survival stories so I'm not so fearful. (And they share great beauty tips too!)

Also, I found wonderful help for understanding mid-life changes in the classic book *Women and Stress* by the late Jean Lush. When I read her list of typical mid-life changes, I thought someone was reading my mind. Symptoms like a drop in energy level, a strange foreboding feeling, the blahs, memory lapses, feelings of failure, daydreaming, and increased introspection[3] all resonated with me. After reading this book I finally feel like I'm not going crazy! I thank God for books which help me navigate life's changes.

I believe God placed me in a job at a high school partly to lessen my anxiety about raising teenagers. I have gotten to know plenty of healthy, happy, well-rounded teens who make wise choices. I have seen several teens recover well from making stupid mistakes. I have learned that many teens are responsible drivers, prudent social media users, sexually pure, and able to stand up to intense peer pressure. Seeing many examples of great teenagers has given me hope and peace for my own family.

I wrote an entire book on the pursuit of peace for the Christmas season. What I learned through writing that book is peace is not possible without Jesus. I am practically guaranteed to get caught up in anxiety's web unless I am spending time every day cultivating my relationship with God. I also learned that God calls us to share peace. Our world is in desperate need of peaceful examples. Bearing the fruit of peace is so important not only for our own sakes, but also for the benefit of others.

God's way

Repeatedly, the Bible tells us not to be afraid or worried. God must have known we would face many anxieties, and that's why his Word is filled with helpful, comforting verses like these:

Search me, O God, and know my heart; test me and know my anxious thoughts. Psalm 139:23

Don't worry about anything; instead, pray about everything. Tell God what you need, and thank him for all he has done. Then you will experience God's peace, which exceeds anything we can understand. His peace will guard your hearts and minds as you live in Christ Jesus. Philippians 4:6-7

It is useless for you to work so hard from early morning until late at night, anxiously working for food to eat; for God gives rest to his loved ones. Psalm 127:2

I learn much about who God is from these verses, and how he wants me to handle my anxieties.

- **All-knowing.** He can see every anxious thought, even the ones I deny or ignore. He can bring my hidden sins to light and grant me comfort, because he knows me through and through. He wants me to open my heart to his search for anxiety.
- **All-hearing.** Every prayer I offer up in a moment of anxiety is heard by God. He longs for me to tell him about everything that worries me. He wants to grant me peace, and he wants me to ask for it through prayer.
- **Peace-giving.** God desires peace in my heart. He grants peace and rest during my anxious striving. As the verse in the

chapter heading states, he wants me to live a peaceful life rather than a life filled with stress and constant anxiety. And as the verse in Philippians states, as I live my life abiding in Christ, he will guard my heart and mind with peace.

Jesus' example

Worry was a huge concern in Jesus' time, just as it is now. Jesus spoke specifically about worry in the Sermon on the Mount in Matthew 6:25-34:

"That is why I tell you not to worry about everyday life—whether you have enough food and drink, or enough clothes to wear. Isn't life more than food, and your body more than clothing? Look at the birds. They don't plant or harvest or store food in barns, for your heavenly Father feeds them. And aren't you far more valuable to him than they are? Can all your worries add a single moment to your life?

"And why worry about your clothing? Look at the lilies of the field and how they grow. They don't work or make their clothing, yet Solomon in all his glory was not dressed as beautifully as they are. And if God cares so wonderfully for wildflowers that are here today and thrown into the fire tomorrow, he will certainly care for you. Why do you have so little faith?

"So don't worry about these things, saying, 'What will we eat? What will we drink? What will we wear?' These things dominate the thoughts of unbelievers, but your heavenly Father already knows all your needs. Seek the Kingdom of God above all else, and live righteously, and he will give you everything you need.

"So don't worry about tomorrow, for tomorrow will bring its own worries. Today's trouble is enough for today."

As busy as Jesus was, he never showed signs of anxiety. He taught the crowds and ministered to thousands, but he didn't exhibit the harried stress with which I'm so familiar. Jesus trusted his Father to provide everything he needed for his ministry. He stayed close to his Father, withdrawing to pray regularly, which connected him to perfect Peace.

These words from the Sermon on the Mount have always brought me comfort in times of anxiety. I turn to them often when financial trials mount. I remember reading them one year when we either needed to sell a spec house or drain our savings account. I read these verses aloud, watching the birds gather to eat sunflower seeds on my porch. I looked outside at the lawn where the dandelions multiplied with abandon. I pondered how Jesus' words are still true today.

If goldfinches can find food without worry, and dandelions can bloom without fear, I can lay my worry aside and trust God to grant me peace.

Holy Spirit's empowerment

The Holy Spirit is a harbinger of peace. On the night of his last supper with his disciples, Jesus promised to send the Holy Spirit in his absence. He said the Holy Spirit would be a teacher and remind them of everything he said. Then Jesus said,

I am leaving you with a gift—peace of mind and heart. And the peace I give is a gift the world cannot give. So do not be troubled or afraid.
John 14:27

This peace is the kind that "passes all understanding" (Philippians 4:7 NIV), available only through the power of the Holy Spirit. Don't you want that kind of peace in your life? Ask the Holy Spirit to give it to you. When you are feeling anxious, pray right then for God to give you his perfect, supernatural peace. He will help you bear the fruit of peace when you walk closely beside him.

Prayer:

Heavenly Father, I want to become a peacemaker, not one trapped in the web of anxiety. Show me the areas of worry inside my heart, areas I don't even recognize. Help me see worry as a sin, because it means I don't fully trust you. Teach me how to choose your peace when I feel anxiety rising. Help me memorize verses on peace so I can recall them instantly when I begin to worry. Jesus, I am trusting you to serve as my Prince of Peace. Empower me through your Holy Spirit to bear the fruit of peace. In Jesus' name, Amen.

Questions for Study and Reflection:
What one change can you make today for a more peaceful, pure, and blameless life?

Pray, Pray, Pray More Worry Less

When you choose from the three passages under "God's Way," which verse resonates most with you, and why?

Philippians 4:6-7

Chapter 4: Impatient or Patient

Better to be patient than powerful; better to have self-control than to conquer a city.
Proverbs 16:32

I used to think of myself as a patient person until I took a hard look at my everyday life.

When I'm driving, I typically don't go over the speed limit. I try to match my driving speed to the speed limit everywhere, whether it's 25 mph or 70 mph.

When someone goes under the speed limit in front of me, I huff and puff and wish they would hurry up and get going. This happens almost every day on my way to work. It's highly likely the drivers in front of me will travel 40 mph in the 55 mph speed limit stretch.

Of course, this happens to be a non-passing zone on a busy two-lane highway, so I'm stuck behind them. I fail the patience test almost daily, muttering under my breath and moving from 0 to 60 mph in one second on the impatience scale.

Waiting in checkout lines is almost as bad. I hide my frustration better when I'm in front of my children. I don't verbally snap at anyone, but I'm sure my body language betrays my impatience. Slow restaurant service irks my patience too. I have fallen prey to this fast-paced, on-demand culture we inhabit. I want it now, please. Right. Now.

If there is one area where my patience fails most, I'm sad to say it's with my children. Is your head nodding? I hope so, because I'm about to sound like a bad mom, and I hope you will give me grace if you've been where I've been.

When I look back on when my children were younger, I cringe remembering how impatient I was when they picked up their toys, put their clothing away, and cleaned up their rooms. Many tears were shed on both sides. Many prayers were sent upward like arrows. Many apologies were offered, asking for forgiveness.

I wish I hadn't yelled so often. I wish I hadn't given those hard stares and spoken those harsh words. I wish I had granted them more grace when they were overwhelmed by large tasks. I could have broken those cleanup projects into 15 minutes at a time instead of dragging them over hours. I regret not instituting a regular pattern of daily pickup, rather than letting work pile up and grow monster-sized. (Just realized I need to apply the daily pickup technique to my own messes!)

However, I am improving with age. Recently my daughter was struggling to put on her orthodontic headgear. In her frustration, she was crying to the point of blubbering. Her hands were slick with tears and saliva, making the job of pulling rubber bands nearly impossible. I wanted so badly to grab the bands and put them on myself. The dark side of me nearly snatched the bands out of her hands in an angry, critical fashion. But I took a deep breath and encouraged her to try again until she got it right. I knew she needed to learn how to do it all by herself. My impatient outburst would only light a fire in a tense situation. After ten tries the bands finally slid into place. I praised her profusely, and I patted myself on the back too. For once, I didn't lose patience with my child.

With my precious children, I am learning my impatience stems from a desire to control the situation at hand. Too many times I have chosen a desire for a clean room over a warm, loving relationship. Too many times I have wanted closure and completion more than I wanted closeness.

As the verse says, it's better to be patient than powerful. It's better to have a slightly messy house and happy children. It's better for me to be a calm, nurturing mom who doesn't vacuum every day than a power-mongering parent with pristine floors.

Meg Meeker offers this insight in her book *Strong Mothers, Strong Sons*, which I feel applies just as well to raising daughters:

It's difficult for mothers to stay patient with our sons, and with ourselves…But the rules are changing all the time, because as our sons grow older, the circumstances change. It's hard to be the first-time parent of a toddler. It's equally hard to be the first-time parent of a teenager…Every stage of development, every battle, every temper tantrum, and every breakup with a girlfriend requires a new batch of patience from us.[4]

I need a fresh batch of patience from the Holy Spirit every day. How about you?

I am entering the parenting phase when my children are gaining lots of life skills and will fail many times before they get it right.

Cooking. Cleaning. Laundry. Passing tests. Driving. Dating (!).

When my impatience threatens, I must remember my own fumbles during those tween and teen years before I got it (mostly) right. If I'm impatient, my children will not enjoy my company and I will push them away. Also, if I'm impatient I will miss out on the chance to teach my children how to grow in patience during learning phases.

I am entering a phase in my writing career when I will make public blunders while I'm learning the steep curve toward traditional publishing (I hope). I can either learn to be patient with myself and move forward or beat myself up and move backward with impatience.

I am ready to grow in patience and set my impatient, demanding, controlling tendencies aside. Toward my family. Toward waitresses and cashiers. Toward slow drivers. Even toward myself, when I don't get it right in record timing.

God's way

Recently I was reading about the Israelites' exodus from Egypt. These people saw the plagues descend on Egyptian homes, saw the death angel take each Egyptian firstborn son, and saw the parting of the Red Sea so they could cross on dry land. They saw the Egyptian army destroyed by crashing waters. They saw manna fall from heaven, quail fly in from nowhere, and water flow from a rock. They even saw God's presence in the form of a cloud.

After all the mighty acts of God they had seen, they grew impatient when Moses stayed up on the mountain longer than they expected. Their impatience created a craving for a false god in the form of a golden calf.

Amazingly, God listened to Moses' plea not to destroy the Israelites for their grave sin. God exacted some immediate costs. He allowed 3,000 people to die, and he stopped traveling with them. They lost fellowship with God due to impatience and rebellion. Yet, God's mercy and perfect patience with his people persisted for many hundreds of years before he exiled them from his presence.

God is perfectly patient. He is slow to anger and loving, and here's his motive:

The Lord really isn't being slow about his promise, as some people think. No, he is being patient for your sake. He does not want anyone to be destroyed, but wants everyone to repent.
2 Peter 3:9

I want to take God's way and make it my own. I want to grow in patience out of concern for others, because I want the best for them. God's patience is others-focused, and mine must be too.

Jesus' example

Can you imagine how tempted Jesus must have been toward impatience and frustration with his disciples? They squabbled amongst themselves, showed unfair judgment of people Jesus loved, and didn't understand Jesus' teachings. As in this example:

While everyone was marveling at everything he was doing, Jesus said to his disciples, "Listen to me and remember what I say. The Son of Man is going to be betrayed into the hands of his enemies." But they didn't know what he meant. Its significance was hidden from them, so they couldn't understand it, and they were afraid to ask him about it.
Luke 9:43-45

Later, on the night of his last supper, this scene unfolded after three years of walking together:

Then his disciples said, "At last you are speaking plainly and not figuratively. Now we understand that you know everything, and there's no need to question you. From this we believe that you came from God."
Jesus asked, "Do you finally believe?" John 16:29-31

When I read these passages, I don't sense frustration or impatience in Jesus' words. He knew their understanding was limited by God's timing. He knew the Holy Spirit would come and open their minds at Pentecost. Yet in Jesus' words, I hear a plaintive longing. I hear an invitation.

Do you finally believe? he asks me. I sense him saying, *After all the good you've seen me do in your life, Sarah, do you finally trust me with everything?* He has been there all along, patiently waiting for my loving, trusting response. His everlasting patience disarms me and pulls me in.

Holy Spirit's empowerment

I have heard many people jokingly quip, "If you pray for patience, that's a prayer God is sure to answer." I think many people avoid praying for patience because they know how impatient they already are, and they don't want any more tests. They don't want any more mirrors held up to their sin of impatience.

I am one of those people! And yet, after writing this chapter, I realize I DO want to bear more patient fruit. My impatience is hurting my relationships with loved ones and dimming the light of Jesus to strangers.

Romans 8:6 states, "...letting the Spirit control your mind leads to life and peace." If I pray for the Holy Spirit to take control of my mind, especially control of my impatient thoughts, I'll be further along the path toward a peaceful life.

I will ask the Holy Spirit to grant me his perfect patience in those times when I feel the huffs and puffs building pressure inside. Those impatient feelings will be my call to prayer from now on.

Prayer:

Heavenly Father, I want to be patient, not bound to impatience. Show me the ways I become impatient every day. Help me see impatience as a sin, because it means I desire control over relationship and obedience. Teach me to put on your patience when I feel impatience pressing close. Jesus, I am trusting you to serve as my example of waiting well. Empower me through your Holy Spirit to bear the fruit of patience. In Jesus' name, Amen.

Questions for Study and Reflection:
Read Proverbs 16:32. How are your impatient moments really grabs for more power?

Think of the situation which triggers impatience in you most often. What kind of plan can you develop for committing this matter to prayer?

Chapter 5: Selfish or Kind

Since God chose you to be the holy people he loves,
you must clothe yourselves with tenderhearted
mercy, kindness, humility, gentleness, and patience.
Colossians 3:12

I must admit, I really like things done my own way
in my home.

I want dishes loaded in the dishwasher a certain
way. I want non-dishwasher dishes (yes, there IS a
difference) hand-washed in a certain order. I want
certain towels in certain locations, some for
decoration and some for use. Even though I'm not
a clean freak, I'm borderline OCD about how
certain things are done certain ways. And I'm
driving my family bonkers with my self-important
rules.

I don't think of myself as pathologically selfish, but
I know I have deep pockets of selfishness just like
everyone else. I really like to spend time alone
thinking, reading, and creating. I have excellent
focus, which is ideal for writing books and creating
art.

But the ability to focus becomes a detriment when
I shut out people I love.

Sometimes I am so focused it's hard to stop what I'm doing, even when one of my children expresses a legitimate need. At times they've stopped asking for my help, and when I realize it, I feel convicted. My selfishness in doing what I want gets in the way of serving my family.

Kindness is intentionally others-focused, not self-focused. Let me be honest here as I administer an antidote to my own selfishness. Kindness is playing games with my children when I would rather be reading. It's cooking foods they prefer, listening to their favorite music in the car, and going to see movies they like. It's giving my husband back scratches when I'm not in the mood for anything but sleep. It's carving out a date night on a weekend reserved for writing. Kindness is being AWARE of my loved ones' needs and treating them the way I'd like to be treated. Especially when I'm all set up to do my own thing.

This morning I watched a video from Ann Voskamp's series on her book, *The Broken Way*. Her quote on loving like Jesus resonated with me, and I think kindness can be swapped for love in the quote too:

"Love is the willingness to be inconvenienced and interrupted."

Kindness which springs from others-focused love looks like this, when I feel inconvenienced and interrupted:

- Getting up from my writing desk to hug my husband before he leaves each morning, because I need to put him first
- Respecting my oldest son's need for more time alone, even when I long for his company, because he needs privacy as a budding teen
- Taking time to snuggle with my middle child every night when I'm tired, because he craves physical affection
- Giving my daughter eye-contact-based attention every day when I'm busy with chores, because she loves focused attention

I recently signed up to take a 30-Day Kindness Challenge—you can sign up too at jointhekindnesschallenge.com. You can choose to customize it for a certain person, or just anyone.

I chose "anyone" because I'm dealing with a situation that's a bit too private to share here. Suffice it to say I really need to focus on being kind in this situation when I want to turn my cheek and give what's not being offered to me.

In this past week or so of the Kindness Challenge, I discovered an ugly self-truth: I resist showing kindness in this difficult situation because I'm steeped in selfishness.

My selfish side wants to complain, lament, recount the wrongs, and be set in my own opinion. My selfish side doesn't even want to consider neutral ground, much less act with kindness.

On the first day of the challenge, I had to promise not to say ANYTHING negative about the other person for 30 days. Wow, that was a reality check! I had been spewing unkind words for *months* without acknowledging my sin.

What I'm doing differently now is venting solely to God. He can handle my raw honesty without being negatively influenced, unlike my husband and closest friends. By keeping my mouth shut toward others and opening it only in God's presence, my faith is growing quickly. I'm learning what's worth arguing about and what's not. I'm learning that God sees the wrongs done to me, and He is my avenger. My trust in Him is getting stronger, since I'm venting upward instead of outward.

I am trying to look for ways to say kind words rather than saying nothing at all. I don't want to fall back into my ingrained pattern of withdrawal. I want to grow in wisdom and use kindness to soothe tensions. God will teach me creative ways to show kindness in this tricky situation as I stay close by His side.

This thought on kindness from Karen Ehman gives me pause:

So just what is God's whole point of us being kind— especially to those who might be different from us or even difficult to love? I believe it is this: because our kindness can be a conduit to help others to discover God's grace and accept his salvation. That is it.[5]

When I look at kindness from that perspective, I realize kindness can be my primary missional effort. As Jesus said, God notices and appreciates small acts of kindness like offering someone a cup of cold water. (Mark 9:41) Who knows if the cup of water I offer may be the conduit of salvation in one person's story? I need to show kindness in all kinds of ways, because I never know how God will use my act of kindness to shape someone's life for the better.

God's way

Consider these vignettes of God's kindness:
He has shown kindness by giving you rain from heaven and crops in their seasons; he provides you with plenty of food and fills your hearts with joy. Acts 14:17 NIV

God's kindness is for everyone. He provides beauty, nourishment, shelter, rest, leisure, and relationships for all mankind. You don't have to be a Christian to experience God's kindness.

Don't you see how wonderfully kind, tolerant, and patient God is with you? Does this mean nothing to you? Can't you see that his kindness is intended to turn you from your sin? Romans 2:4

God's kindness has a specific purpose. He wants to win hearts to himself by showing kindness. He wants us to be his own people. As the verse in the chapter heading states, kindness is only one of the virtues he wishes for us to display.

And God raised us up with Christ and seated us with him in the heavenly realms in Christ Jesus, in order that in the coming ages he might show the incomparable riches of his grace, expressed in his kindness to us in Christ Jesus. Ephesians 2:6-7 NIV

God's kindness connects us to Jesus. Jesus' life and sacrifice were the ultimate expression of God's love and kindness to all of us. Jesus makes it possible for us to experience God's eternal riches, including his perfect kindness.

Jesus' example

The Bible tells many stories of Jesus' kind treatment of others. The one I want to discuss here is his meeting with the woman at the well in John 4.

This woman had several strikes against her. First, she was a female in a time when men dominated, and women were marginalized. She was a Samaritan, a race standing in bitter opposition to the Jews. She was living in sin and had a checkered past.

This woman was drawing water at a well in the middle of the day, when the square was empty, and she wouldn't face the whispers and judgment. She was living with shame and despondency.

Jesus looked right past all these problems. He reached out in kindness, asking her for a drink. His simple request initiated a powerful discussion, reaching deep into her heart. He called her "dear" (vs. 21) and told her he could give her living water that would last (vs. 14). And then, he revealed himself as the Messiah to this woman no one else considered worthy of attention (vs. 26).

This woman's life was instantly changed by Jesus' kindness. She ran back to the village without her water jug, casting aside her reticence to tell everyone she had met Jesus.

I want my acts of kindness to have that kind of power. I want to notice the quiet people, the lonely people, and the marginalized people in our culture and reach out to them with the same kindness Jesus showed to the woman at the well.

Holy Spirit's empowerment

I can ask the Holy Spirit to open my eyes to kindness opportunities. Ann Voskamp shares several ideas in *The Broken Way*, such as baking brownies for neighbors and leaving dollars on shelves at a convenience store for people to buy little treats. The Holy Spirit can open my eyes to needs for kindness and how to fill them in practical ways like these.

I've gotten several more ideas from joining the Kindness Challenge too. It's not that there's a shortage of ideas stopping the kindness flow. It's my lack of willingness to be others-focused, interrupted, and inconvenienced. I want to pray for the Holy Spirit to overcome my selfishness in those areas.

In fact, I will pray specifically for prompts toward kindness in those moments.

When I'm writing on a deadline, I'm going to look for ways to bear the fruit of kindness in those interrupted moments.

When I'm busy at work, I'm going to pray for the fruit of kindness to show through me in moments of inconvenience. This is not the type of prayer I typically pray. But this prayer may be the kind I need to pray to allow the Holy Spirit to work through me in new ways, so new fruit can be shared.

Prayer:

*Heavenly Father, I want to be kind instead of selfish.
Show me the ways I am blind to my own selfishness.
Help me see my selfishness as sin, because it means I
trust myself more than I trust you. Teach me to
show your kindness when I am tempted to do my
own thing my own way. Jesus, I am trusting you to
serve as my example of others-focused kindness.
Empower me through your Holy Spirit to bear the
fruit of kindness. In Jesus' name, Amen.*

Questions for Study and Reflection:
How willing are you to be inconvenienced and
interrupted?

Read through the story of the woman at the well in
John 4. How are Jesus' words to the woman a good
model of kindness for you?

Chapter 6: Worldly or Good

For this light within you produces only what is good
and right and true.
Ephesians 5:9

I read many blogs each week along with several
popular magazines. The visuals delight me, along
with the promise of all kinds of new things. Pretty
things, slick things, and seemingly perfect things to
fill up my secret, insatiable greed inside called
worldliness.

How does the world entice you?

Advertising hooks me. I've worked in advertising
and I understand the methods of speaking to pain
points: This thing will bring you satisfaction. This
thing will make life easier. This thing will soothe
your hurts.

Sometimes that's true. Advertising helps me find
new books, new tools, and new remedies I
wouldn't have discovered on my own. These new
things really do improve my quality of life, and I'm
grateful.

Yet it's all too easy for me to fall into a worldly
trap when I feast on too much advertising.
Thoughts like the following run through my mind:
I need this. I deserve this. I can't live without this.

Thoughts like these probably ran through Eve's mind before she grabbed the forbidden fruit in the Garden of Eden. Worldliness whispered to her as it does to us every day.

Worldliness says, *Stuff will fill this hole inside me.*

Enough stuff will free me from my needs.

I don't like feeling needy.

God says He's enough, but I'm not sure if that's true.

Don't you dare take my stuff away!

Whispers call to me from these traps: books, clothing, food, art supplies, plants, and décor. Anything in the clearance aisle is hard for me to pass up, especially when I have a 15% off coupon to boot. I have a whole closet of stuff I haven't even used yet, because I worshiped the idol called Deal.

It's so hard to resist the pull of worldliness! Maybe you have issues with other idols. Maybe celebrity gossip calls your name. Maybe soapy television shows or movies seduce you. Maybe you can't resist technology, alcohol, gossip, or buying lottery tickets every week. Maybe you are obsessed over sports or fashion or redecorating. Are you tired of getting caught in multiple worldly traps as much as I am?

Trying to get rid of worldliness alone is kind of like going on a diet.

At first, you make healthy choices in the hopes of instant results. Whether you're giving up carbs, alcohol, shopping, or watching soap operas, it's the same. You think, "I'll just stop for a week and I'll feel better right away." A few days go by without your fix and you can handle it. You give in just once and get hooked again. Then you become overwhelmed and discouraged. You go back to your old ways, feeling guilty and despondent. Sooner or later, the cycle repeats.

This is worldliness detox based on willpower, and that's why it fails just like dieting.

Goodness is powered by the Holy Spirit. Goodness edifies, builds up, and heals. Goodness fills up that inside hole completely, without greed. Goodness is God-powered, not self-powered.

With the Holy Spirit's help, you can have a new life with goodness.

Goodness can help you choose edifying food, makeup, clothing, books, movies, décor, even thoughts and words. Once you taste goodness, worldliness loses its strong appeal.

I recently read a book by Michelle Brown titled *Energy Reset.* One of the powerful truths this book taught me is that health stems from our gut.

Our intestines are the powerful highway for sending goodness to all other body parts. When we consume non-edifying food, our whole body suffers in ways we don't even recognize. When we consume edifying food, the whole body benefits.

What I'm trying in my own personal Energy Reset is cutting sugar, gluten, and dairy out of breakfast, lunch, and snacks for 30 days. I'm sure when I get on track with this Energy Reset, foods which once tasted so good will taste too rich or too sweet. Strawberries in the raw will taste so much better and do much more good than strawberry-filled pastries, for example.

I want to adjust my tastes, so goodness is my natural preference to worldliness, in food and in all other areas. I can't do this alone; I must rely on the Holy Spirit to hold me accountable and teach me new ways of living and bearing better fruit.

God's way

In the original creation not yet marred by sin, goodness abounded.

Yet God still created Adam and Eve with needs. They needed food and rest. They needed work, which God provided. They needed companionship and love. They needed time with God every day. Adam and Eve were created to be dependent. They didn't mind their dependence on God until Satan deceived them into believing it wasn't good.

He tricked them into believing the knowledge of good AND evil was better than knowing only good (Genesis 3:5). He is the "ruler of this world" (John 12:31) and he enticed them to worldliness.

God created a world of goodness, and it was enough. It was more than enough. Adam and Eve didn't believe that, just like we don't believe that God really wants what's best for us.

1 John 2:15, 17 offers God's view of worldliness:

Do not love this world nor the things it offers you, for when you love the world, you do not have the love of the Father in you...And this world is fading away, along with everything that people crave. But anyone who does what pleases God will live forever.

God has the long view; worldliness presents a short view. God wants us to value what lasts into eternity more than we value the temporary pleasures of this world.

Jesus' example

If you are reading this book, your income level is likely in the top 5% of the world's wealthiest people.

On most days that's hard for me to believe, but it's true. I have more in common with the rich man in Matthew 19 than I care to admit.

This young man approached Jesus, asking what he needed to do to secure salvation. Jesus said he needed to obey the commandments. The man said he had lived a righteous life and wanted to know what else he needed to do.

Then Jesus said, "If you want to be perfect, go and sell all your possessions and give the money to the poor, and you will have treasure in heaven. Then come, follow me." Matthew 19:21

The Bible says the man walked away in sadness because he was wealthy. He didn't want to give up his wealth to follow Jesus.

I am not saying that all of us need to liquidate our holdings and give everything to the poor. What I am saying is Jesus' statement to his disciples when the man walked away gives me pause as a member of the top 5%:

I tell you the truth, it is very hard for a rich person to enter the Kingdom of Heaven. I'll say it again—it is easier for a camel to go through the eye of a needle than for a rich person to enter the Kingdom of God! Matthew 19:23-24

I want to hold my possessions loosely, so they don't exert such power over me. I want to give and share more freely.

I want to recognize the wealth I've been given and see how it can benefit others in the 95% bracket. I don't want worldliness to hold me back from the best God's kingdom offers in this life or the next.

I also notice that Jesus experienced goodness by enjoying time with people. He celebrated with friends at the wedding at Cana. The home of Mary, Martha, and Lazarus was a regular stop on his circuit.

The good life to Jesus was feasting on the fellowship of his friends. He was never caught up in the trappings of this world. He made people his primary focus, connecting with them in intentional, personal, and meaningful interactions.

Jesus also put goodness in action. He healed the sick, restored sight to the blind, and raised people from the dead. His example inspires me to not just say good things but do good things to bless others and quench their spiritual thirst.

Holy Spirit's empowerment

I want my heart to have the good soil in the parable of the soils in Matthew 13. Good soil produces the largest harvest. Good soil is nourishing, well-watered, and loose, providing the best possible environment for seeds to grow.

I am asking the Holy Spirit to pull out the rocks and thorns of worldliness that stunt my potential for growth. I am asking him to use the rain of hard times to soften my soil and make it workable for planting. I am asking the Holy Spirit for favorable conditions, so I can bear a harvest of goodness for God's glory.

Ask the Holy Spirit to help you choose the good life. Not the flashy, elusive, worldly life, but the best life for you. Ask him to help you do good deeds for others out of the goodness he supplies to your heart.

Prayer:

Heavenly Father, I want to be good instead of worldly. Show me the ways I ignore and hide my worldly tendencies. Help me see my worldliness as sin, because it means I despise my dependence on you. Teach me to choose goodness when I am tempted to choose what's temporal. Jesus, I am trusting you to serve as my example of living the good life. Empower me through your Holy Spirit to bear the fruit of goodness. In Jesus' name, Amen.

Questions for Study and Reflection:

Read 1 John 5:16. Which craving of yours comes to mind when you read this verse?

Read Ephesians 5:1-20. How can the Holy Spirit help you resist worldly enticements?

Chapter 7: Harsh or Gentle

*A gentle answer deflects anger, but harsh words
make tempers flare.*
Proverbs 15:1

If you ask friends and family to describe me in a
phrase or two, I guarantee one of the most popular
answers would be "honest to a fault."

Honesty delivered gently is refreshing and
winsome. Honesty delivered harshly is painful
and offensive.

When I look back on times I have been harshest in
my responses, those were the times I felt most
unloved. The lack of love caused anger and hurt to
fester inside, and hot lava boiled up through my
harsh tones and words.

Until two years ago, I lived my life as a mostly
unhappy person. I was codependent and
emotionally abused, passive and frustrated.

Happiness seemed so far out of reach, even though
I was a Christian. Through a long, painful healing
process, I changed old dynamics and finally found
happiness in most of my days.

This may sound silly, but I'm still learning how happy feels. Harsh is more familiar. Harsh is how I was treated for decades. Harsh is how I sounded.

I used to be so harsh in my judgment of others. I was unfriendly, suspicious, and paranoid.

Emotional abuse will shape you to feel that way about everyone, even people who want to help.

I used to be so harsh with my children. I laid down the law so often, not granting enough grace. If they followed the rules, I felt like Supermom. But if they crossed me, I became Queen of Harsh.

I used to be so harsh with my husband. I nitpicked, nagged, and criticized. I expected too much and didn't accept him for who he is, faults and all. My harshness toward him sparked fires and created distance in our marriage.

Happy feels good now. Happy is such a contrast to those harsh days. Now that I'm becoming more familiar with happiness, I recognize harshness much faster. And I'm able to replace it with gentleness, now that God has healed me.

I used to be harsh because I thought gentle was weak. I confused gentleness with passivity, and passivity hasn't done me any favors. I had to learn that gentleness is really strength reigned in.

Chuck Swindoll describes gentleness this way:

...gentleness includes such enviable qualities as having strength under control, being calm and peaceful when surrounded by a heated atmosphere, emitting a soothing effect on those who may be angry or otherwise beside themselves, and possessing tact and gracious courtesy that causes others to retain their self-esteem and dignity.[6]

When I see gentleness like that, I want it so much for myself. I want to treat my husband and children with the gentleness of grace. I want to carefully consider my words and tone before I speak, because I want to exhibit tact and courtesy. I want my natural honesty to be tempered with gentleness, which will soothe others and draw them closer to Christ.

The book of James is famous for its chapter on controlling the tongue. James likens the tongue to "a tiny spark [that] can set a great forest on fire" (James 3:5). Gentleness begins by controlling the tongue. James warns against praises and curses flowing from the same mouth (3:10). I confess I have made that mistake many times, sometimes without realizing it, other times fully knowing I would inflict pain.

Gentleness is soothing, not wounding. That's how I want my words to sound.

I want to be gentle with harsh people. They are coming from hurt places, just as I was. Perhaps God will use my gentleness to speak into their hearts. I want my answers to deflect anger and settle things down. This requires a close dependence on the Holy Spirit. I want him to guide my words and convict me BEFORE I say something harsh.

God's way

God was gentle with a woman named Hagar in Genesis 16. Abram and Sarai were unable to bear children. Sarai proposed to Abram that he sleep with her servant Hagar to conceive an heir. Hagar became pregnant and treated Sarai with contempt...doesn't this sound like a modern-day story between two feuding women? Then Sarai complained about Hagar to Abram. He let Sarai take charge of the situation, and "Sarai treated Hagar so harshly that she finally ran away" (Genesis 16:6).

Sarai's harshness caused division and strife. Remember, it was her bad idea in the first place to get Hagar and Abram together. But instead of taking responsibility for her actions, she grasped at harshness to regain a semblance of power. God was gentle with Hagar when Sarai was harsh. He sent an angel to Hagar in the wilderness, encouraging her to return home. After that encounter, she called God "The One Who Sees Me," likely because she felt unseen in her situation.

Years later, when another child was born to renamed Abraham and Sarah, Hagar and her son were cast out for good. But God dealt gently with Hagar again. He called to Hagar from heaven, strengthening and comforting her in her harsh environment. He even extended a promise of many descendants to her family line.

God is gentle with us when we don't deserve it. Hagar didn't really deserve God's kindness. She was a foreigner, outside of the family of God's people, and she treated Sarai with contempt. But God saw her, cared about her, and provided for her all the same. Just as he does for all of us.

He does not punish us for all our sins; he does not deal harshly with us, as we deserve. Psalm 103:10

If I want to be more like God, I must choose to deal gently with people even when they don't deserve it.

Jesus' example

One day the religious leaders brought a woman to Jesus. They had dragged her from her bed of adultery and put her shame, fear, and humiliation on display in front of the crowd. They wanted Jesus to vindicate their desire to stone her, based on the law. The leaders were using this woman as a pawn to try and trap Jesus.

As the Son of God, Jesus had more rights to judge and condemn this woman than the religious leaders. He had the right to come down on her harsh and swift. He had the right to cast the first stone.

Yet he silently, mysteriously wrote in the dust while the leaders pressured him for an answer. Finally, Jesus said, "All right, but let the one who has never sinned throw the first stone!" (John 8:7)

He knew he was the only one without sin there. The only one with the right to cast the stone. But he withheld his right. He chose to be gentle instead of harsh, when everyone else was poised for harsh treatment.

Everyone walked away until Jesus was left alone with this poor, frightened, wretched woman. When he finally spoke, this scene unfolded.

"Where are your accusers? Didn't even one of them condemn you?"
"No, Lord," she said.
And Jesus said, "Neither do I. Go and sin no more."
John 8:10-11

Do you hear the gentleness in his voice? He didn't sugarcoat her sin, but he didn't wave it in her face either. He didn't condemn her when he had every right to do so.

How many times have I been harsh to someone who needed gentleness? How many times have I been quick to judge and cast verbal stones? I want to be like Jesus, who didn't fall into the harshness trap. I want to show the world the quiet power of gentleness.

Holy Spirit's empowerment

As we've learned, harshness comes from the tongue. Ask the Holy Spirit to help you watch your words. Memorize this scripture and pray it often:

Take control of what I say, O Lord, and guard my lips. Psalm 141:3

Remember that Matthew 12:36 says we will give an account for every word we speak, including our harsh words. Let's be different from the rest of the world. Let us have speech free from harshness but full of gentleness. Let's bear the fruit of a "gentle and quiet spirit" (1 Peter 3:4) through the power of the Holy Spirit.

Prayer:

Heavenly Father, I want to be gentle instead of harsh. Show me the ways I am unaware of how harsh I can be. Help me see my harshness as sin, because it means I want the power that only belongs to you. Teach me to show your gentleness when I am tempted to speak without thinking. Jesus, I am trusting you to serve as my example of strength under restraint. Empower me through your Holy Spirit to bear the fruit of gentleness. In Jesus' name, Amen.

Questions for Study and Reflection:

Read Proverbs 15:1. In what ways have you seen both sides of this verse prove to be true?

Who needs your gentle treatment, even if you feel they don't deserve it?

Chapter 8: Scattered or Faithful

For if we are faithful to the end, trusting God just as firmly as when we first believed, we will share in all that belongs to Christ.
Hebrews 3:14

In this stage of my life, I feel pulled in so many different directions.

My children are old enough to take care of themselves most of the time, but none of them are old enough to drive. They have way fewer extracurricular activities than their peers, yet the miles continue to rack up on the minivan odometer. Practices, games, church events, and playdates keep us going every day.

The older my children get, the faster life speeds by in a blur. The beginning of school year bleeds right into Thanksgiving, as activities pile up each autumn weekend. December whizzes by with parties, programs, and gatherings; it's over almost as soon as it begins. We catch our breath between basketball and baseball seasons, then spring practices push us right into Memorial Day.

I live for summer's slower pace.

Most days I feel scattered. If I don't write everything down or do a task right when it's in front of me, disaster strikes. A bill doesn't get paid. The cat doesn't get fed, so she climbs up in the attic and must be extracted by hand. The meat isn't taken out of the freezer to thaw, so we eat frozen dinners, again. Mornings are frazzled. Evenings press tight with responsibility mixed with exhaustion. I pray for a snow day, even when the ten-day forecast predicts spring-like temperatures.

It's easy to drop healthy commitments when I feel scattered.   Especially exercise, eating right, family devotions, and keeping up with friends. All the things most beneficial to my well-being tend to go first.

Alli Worthington writes in her book *Breaking Busy*:

If you are unfamiliar with the phrase "tyranny of the urgent," it describes a life of constant tension between the urgent (constantly putting out little fires and checking off the to-do lists) and the truly important (our relationship with God and the bigger priorities of life). The problem is that many important tasks (such as getting adequate sleep, spending quiet time with God every day, and working toward the big goals in life) don't seem urgent enough to demand our immediate attention, while urgent tasks (like stopping the kids from bickering over who gets the toy first or answering that text) aren't always important.[7]

I am dog-tired of being a slave to urgency. And it's showing in procrastination. It's late February and I still need to take down a string of Christmas lights on the back porch railing. I still need to carry some boxes to the basement and sort the contents, which have sat in the living room for a month. Papers are unfiled on multiple counters. Instead of putting my laundry away, I've been grabbing clean socks from a basket for a week. When urgency presses too close, I give up completely, and then I'm discouraged by the messes I create.

What I need is faithfulness. Faithfulness is rhythmical, reliable, and dependable. Faithfulness sets things right.

Faithfulness is taking care of tasks in rational fashion. For example, if I carry my basket of clean, folded clothes 100 steps upstairs, why don't I take five more minutes and put it all away?

Faithfulness follows through. I know this. Yet I allow myself to be scattered by a television show coming on, the pull of a magazine that just came in the mail, or the call of my son to inspect his latest Lego creation. Most of the time, five minutes would make a huge impact in developing more faithful routines. Ten minutes, even better. Fifteen minutes per day just might revolutionize the entire household!

Faithfulness sets traditions and sticks to them. What I want my children to remember is the "we always" moments. When they are grown up, I want them to say, "We always prayed together before our meals. We always had home-cooked suppers on Sundays. We always read devotions before bed. We always hugged each other before we left the house." Faithfulness establishes patterns which are important for family bonding.

Today I sat down to write the last third of this book. Sometimes I resist the pressure of meeting a hard deadline by intentionally allowing myself to get scattered. Immature and silly, I know. I let Facebook notifications, blog comments, and other online distractions pull me away from writing. Realizing four hours had passed without writing a word in here, I finally disconnected from the alluring Internet. Guess what? My writing flourished without those online distractions, because faithfulness requires focus.

I have learned another lesson about faithfulness through writing. One year ago, I began blogging five days per week. Five days per week for 52 weeks yielded a finished memoir manuscript (after six years!), three different blog series, and three self-published Bible studies. That's more writing results than I've produced since I was an English major in college. Fruit is borne from the labor of faithfully working at a goal every day.

God has been faithful to me in so many ways. He has faithfully listened to my prayers and answered many of them. He has provided year after year for all my needs to be met, then blessed me with abundance on top of my needs. He has steadily walked by my side, teaching me his ways and his word. I can mimic God's faithfulness by bearing faithful fruit in the Holy Spirit's power instead of falling into scattered chaos.

God's way

I like this quote from Jen Wilkin about God's eternal nature:

He is never early nor late, never subject to the tyranny of a deadline, never in a hurry, never playing catch-up with a schedule that has careened out of control.[8]

The idea that God never gets in a hurry brings me a deep sense of comfort. I love knowing he is stable, secure, unchanging, and settled. I need that kind of anchor in my life.

But that idea also convicts me. In these ways I am so unlike God, it's a joke. I think my failure stems from my inability to say no, when God has no problem saying no. He is perfectly balanced and owes no one any explanations.

I am frequently out-of-balance and internally pressured to explain myself to everyone. If I'm unable to commit, why do I attach an explanation to my "no"? I worry too much about what others think and not enough about what God thinks about my choices.

This just happened today. I messaged a bunch of acquaintances on Facebook, asking them to vote for me in a contest. My anxious thoughts scattered all over the place while I copied and pasted the message, stretching me thin with anxiety. Thoughts like these swirled: *What if no one responds? What if they unfriend me for asking? What if I sound desperate—what will they think of me?* Those self-conscious thoughts are so far away from what God wants for me.

In a quiet moment a little while later, he spoke to my heart, comforting me with his promises and his unconditional love. His faithful encouragement centered me, grounded me, and brought me back to my best self.

When I listen to God's voice and take time to recount his faithfulness to me, I don't feel scattered anymore. I feel his peace.

Jesus' example

Martha is my scattered sister in Scripture. She is the one who wanted everything perfect but ended up getting it wrong.

I envision Martha like myself before throwing a big party:

- frazzled from too much work and not enough delegation
- sore from using untrained muscles to dust the nooks and crannies
- exhausted from staying up until midnight baking the cake
- irritable because no one cares about the little things as much as I do

I get Martha. She wants a pretty, pristine party. She wants it all to be perfect. Since perfection isn't attainable, the wheels fell off in her pursuit. So, she tried to rope Jesus into her quest for perfection, asking him to direct her sister Mary to stop dawdling and start helping.

Jesus said to Martha,

My dear Martha, you are worried and upset over all these details! There is only one thing worth being concerned about. Mary has discovered it, and it will not be taken away from her. Luke 10:41-42

Jesus calls me to concern myself with only one thing, which is listening to his voice.

I need to listen to his voice first thing in the morning, before my busy day begins.

I need to listen to his voice before I sign my children up for overlapping sports seasons.

I need to listen to his voice first before I commit to anything that interferes with Sabbath rest.

I need to listen to his voice first before I take on a new ministry role—is it for God's glory or my own?

If I listen to Jesus' voice when I feel scattered, he will cultivate greater faithfulness in my life's rhythms.

Holy Spirit's empowerment

In my book *Christmas Peace for Busy Moms*, I wrote extensively about developing peaceful practices to reign in the scattered feeling December often brings. Yet in my own power I cannot adhere to even the best-laid plans without the Holy Spirit's help.

I ask him to hold me accountable for daily Bible study, daily down time, daily connections with my husband and children, and daily tasks. When I'm not in tune with the Holy Spirit, my life scatters very quickly.

I believe we can inspire other scattered people by living a Spirit-led life of faithful rhythms. One area that is begging for faithfulness is the Sabbath. Does your family take one day of rest and leisure every week?

My family instituted the faithful observance of Sunday downtime years ago. It's a pattern which has blessed all five of us with a greater sense of connection.

I challenge you to ask the Holy Spirit to develop faithfulness in observing the Sabbath in your family. You may start a faithfulness revolution among your friends, neighbors, and family members in this scattered culture, so desperate for God's perfect peace.

Prayer:

Heavenly Father, I want to be faithful instead of scattered. Show me the ways I scatter myself without realizing it. Help me see my scattered ways as sin, because you call me to a life of peace and faithfulness. Teach me to show faithfulness when I am tempted to run in ten different directions at once. Jesus, I am trusting you to speak to my heart about the faithful way you want me to follow. Empower me through your Holy Spirit to bear the fruit of faithfulness. In Jesus' name, Amen.

Questions for Study and Reflection:

In what ways have you succumbed to the tyranny of the urgent?

How do Jesus' words to Martha apply to your life?

Chapter 9: Indulgent or Self-Controlled

A person without self-control is like a city with broken-down walls.
Proverbs 25:28

Self-control is the hardest fruit of the spirit for me to bear.

I think it's because self-control is involved in all the other fruits. I must employ self-control to be gentle instead of harsh, good instead of worldly, and patient instead of impatient. If I allow the Holy Spirit to fully take charge of the branch in my heart that bears the fruit of self-control, all the other branches will benefit.

It's hard to admit. My #1 area of indulgence is food.

As I mentioned in Chapter 6, I have a love affair with sugar, dairy, and gluten. I plan to cut these out of my diet for Lent this year. Dairy and gluten will be difficult to give up, but sugar will be my punisher.

Sugar is the first thing to enter my mouth each day. I stir honey into my hot tea and relish the sweet rush. I usually eat something sweet for breakfast, whether it's a smoothie or a granola bar. I snack on something sugary around 10:00 a.m. I like to finish meals with a sweet taste in my mouth, so I have an after-lunch mint or piece of chocolate. My afternoon snack contains another sweet bite, and I finish supper with dessert many nights.

It's time to face facts: I'm addicted to sugar.

Today I tried to cut it out after breakfast. I ate my sweet cinnamon muffin, but then I tried to do without sugar the rest of the day. I ate eggs at 9:00 a.m., a handful of nuts for a snack, and vegetable soup for lunch. Five minutes passed after my last spoonful of soup, and I couldn't stand the strong temptation. Instead of praying for help or distracting myself with a healthy activity, I got a piece of chocolate out of my secret cabinet (so I don't have to share with my children) and gobbled it down.

I couldn't go without sugar for even five minutes after lunch.

How in the world can I go without sugar for 30 days?

I CANNOT do it without God's help!

Referring to the verse in this chapter's heading, Jerry Bridges wrote in *Respectable Sins*:

In biblical times, a city's walls were its chief means of defense. If the walls were breached, an invading army could pour into the city and conquer it...In the same way that a city without walls was vulnerable to an invading army, so a person without self-control is vulnerable to all kinds of temptations.

Despite the scriptural teaching on self-control, I suspect this is one virtue that receives little conscious *attention from most Christians. We have boundaries from our Christian culture that tend to restrain us from obvious sins, but within those boundaries we pretty much live as we please. We seldom say "no" to our desires and emotions. A lack of self-control may well be one of our more "respectable" sins. And because we tolerate this, we become more vulnerable to other "respectable" sins.*[9]

So many Christians like me struggle with the temptation to indulge in food. I think indulging in food is more socially acceptable among Christians than other vices like drinking and smoking, for example. Yet indulgence in this area can lead to tolerance of other sins, as Bridges mentioned. He shared a personal story to illustrate the point:

I think of my own craving for ice cream years ago when I would have a dish of it at dinner and another at bedtime. In that situation, God convicted me of my lack of self-control by causing me to see that a seemingly benign practice greatly weakened my self-control in other more critical areas.[10]

What disturbs me about this story is the question it poses: What other areas of my life are weakened due to my lack of self-control with food?

This is an ugly truth I need to face: I often hear the Holy Spirit speaking to me about food, but I choose to ignore him anyway. He doesn't speak in a shaming voice; he speaks with loving concern. He says things like, "You don't need that chocolate right now," but I wilfully ignore him and give in to indulgence.

What if he has stopped speaking to me in other areas because I'm not willing to obey him in this one?

I don't think God is holding out on me to be mean or to manipulate me. I'm not saying I must give up sugar to earn God's favor either.

What I am saying is since I haven't proven myself trustworthy in this area, God may not entrust me with other responsibilities until I show myself trustworthy in this smaller matter. I treat my children the same way when they have broken my trust.

I have never thought about it that way before.

The parable of the talents in Matthew 25:14-30 has a long history of capturing my attention. Because I was a gifted student in elementary school, I have always identified with the servant given the most talents.

I saw my talents as a serious responsibility. I have never seen myself as the servant given one talent, wasting it by burying it in the ground.

But what if I am the servant with one talent when it comes to my food indulgence? What if I'm afraid to use food in the good way God intended, and I'm burying it in my dark areas of toxic patterns?

Food has long been my comforter where God wanted to step in. Sugar has been my stand-in savior when I was lonely, depressed, rushed, stressed out, and mistreated.

The sugar rush produces a momentary high, lifting me out of my troubles for one moment. Then the sour side effects always follow: excess weight, mouth sores, blood glucose crashes, and the slow, silent damage to my internal organs.

As far back as I can remember, my relationship with food has been messy and complicated.

I want to give up sugar this Lent not because I want to lose weight or eat healthier. I want to give up my food indulgence because it's standing between me and God in ways I don't fully understand.

I don't plan to give it up forever; I want to limit sweets to a reasonable, moderate level of consumption. Not five or more times per day any longer. And I don't want food to stand in for God's comfort any more.

I am asking God to help me reconstruct my broken-down walls this Lent. He can help me build solid walls of self-control based on his word. He will comfort me with his constant presence.

I want to begin the practice of turning to him first instead of things like sugar to fill me up.

God's way

God is perfectly controlled. He never gets out of whack. He never says something he regrets. He never overdoes it or underdoes it. He literally has it all together.

He never indulges, because he doesn't need to. He owns everything. He's not grasping for more than what he already has. Indulging hints at scarcity. *Maybe this pleasure won't be available to me in the future*, I think. So, I grab it up now while it's in front of me, ignoring the consequences.

I like what Jerry Bridges said about God's intent in *The Practice of Godliness*:

There is no doubt that God intends that we enjoy the physical things of this life which he has so graciously provided...But man in his sin has corrupted all of the natural blessings God has given. Because our desires have been corrupted, those things which God intended for our use and enjoyment have a tendency to become our masters.[11]

God's original creation reflected his perfect control and balance. Yet we indulge in his good gifts and allow them to control us rather than reigning over them, as we were called to do in God's original edict (Genesis 1:28). Indulgence began in the Garden of Eden when Eve reached for that sweet fruit. My reach mirrors hers every time I take something good and corrupt its intended use.

Jesus' example

The best example of Jesus' self-control is when he got up early to pray after a very long day of ministry.
The day before, he healed many people, with the whole town gathered to watch (Mark 1:33).
Surely, he was exhausted from so much personal interaction.

But the Bible records this: "Before daybreak the next morning, Jesus got up and went out to an isolated place to pray" (Mark 1:35). Sometimes I wake up an hour before the alarm and turn back over to get more sleep. If that happened to Jesus, he took it as a sign to get up and spend time with his Father in heaven.

Jesus' self-discipline impresses me. He got tired and worn out like the rest of us, and I'm glad the Bible records that for our benefit.

Yet he never forgot what was most important. He was perfectly self-controlled not only because he was divine, but also because his priorities were straight.

If my priorities are in line with God's Word, and I'm following him closely every day, self-control is easier to choose when I feel tempted to indulge.

Holy Spirit's empowerment

In this food challenge I'm facing soon, I will rely heavily on the Holy Spirit.
I will open myself to his promptings to resist temptation. I will pray for strength, focus, and the larger goals. I will pray for greater spiritual truth to be revealed as I fast from the foods I once indulged in so frequently.

Even though I'll be giving up a familiar vice, I trust the Holy Spirit will show me brand-new truths I've never seen before.

As I mentioned, growing in self-control will help every other aspect of spiritual fruit-bearing. I want to grow in all the fruits of the spirit this year.

If I can move forward with self-control, my journey will be even more fruitful. I'm looking forward to seeing what the Holy Spirit will do in my life as I surrender to his ways.

Prayer:

Heavenly Father, I want to be self-controlled instead of indulgent. Show me the pockets of indulgence I hide from public view. Help me see my indulgence as sin, because it means I choose things to stand in the way of a relationship with you. Teach me to practice self-control when I am tempted to indulge in my old habits. Jesus, I am trusting you to serve as my example of perfect discipline. Empower me through your Holy Spirit to bear the fruit of self-control. In Jesus' name, Amen.

Questions for Study and Reflection:
In what area are you most tempted to be indulgent?

How can growing in self-control help you bear more fruit in other areas?

Closing and Bonus Offers

They are like trees planted along the riverbank,
bearing fruit each season. Their leaves never
wither, and they prosper in all they do.
Psalm 1:3

I hope this book has blessed you in a new way. I would love to hear how God has worked in your heart through this study. Please join my Facebook page at **facebook.com/sarahgeringercreates** and let me know how your life is more fruitful because of this study. I look forward to reading your comments!

As a thank you gift for joining me on this journey, **I want to give you a Fruitful Life Prayer Calendar and Study Guide.** I've had a lot of fun putting these free gifts together just for you. Enter your email address in the pink box at **sarahgeringer.com** to unlock these two gifts and receive other free resources.

Sign up in the pink box at **sarahgeringer.com** to receive sneak peeks of my next book while I'm writing it. I hope you will join me on this next journey of finding peace in God's Word.

Your review of this book on Amazon, Goodreads, and other social media will help others bear more fruit for God's kingdom. **Please take a few minutes to post an honest and helpful review.** I deeply appreciate your shares as I work to expand my writing ministry.

Suggest this book to a friend or family member who is looking for fruitfulness and freedom from common sins. You never know whose life may be changed by spreading the word.

May God bless you as you seek to follow him more closely!

Sarah Geringer

About the Author

Sarah Geringer is a devoted follower of Jesus, wife, mother of three, and a writer and artist. She has blogged since 2010, and currently blogs at **sarahgeringer.com.**

Sarah has always loved Bible study. As a child she gained a strong foundation of Bible knowledge through Lutheran education. Sarah self-published *Christmas Peace for Busy Moms* in October 2016 and *Newness of Life* in January 2017.

Sarah holds a Bachelor of Arts in English from Covenant College and a Bachelor of Fine Arts in graphic design and illustration from Southeast Missouri State University. She enjoys reading, drawing and painting, gardening, baking, scrapbooking, journaling, and walking in God's beautiful creation.

Sarah lives with her husband and three children in her beloved home state of Missouri.

Connect with Sarah on her blog and through these other online outlets:

Facebook: facebook.com/sarahgeringercreates
Twitter: @sarahgeringer
Goodreads: goodreads.com/sarah_geringer
Pinterest: pinterest.com/s105
Instagram: @sgeringer

Notes

1. Jen Wilkin, *None Like Him.* (Wheaton, IL: Crossway, 2016), p. 52.
2. Jerry Bridges, *The Practice of Godliness.* (Colorado Springs, CO: Navpress, 1983), p.137.
3. Jean Lush, *Women and Stress.* (Grand Rapids, MI: Revell, 2008), p. 111.
4. Meg Meeker, M. D., *Strong Mothers, Strong Sons.* (New York, NY: Ballantine Books, 2014), p. 94.
5. Karen Ehman, *Listen, Love, Repeat.* (Grand Rapids, MI: Zondervan, 2016), p. 218.
6. Chuck Swindoll, *Improving Your Serve.* (Nashville, TN: Thomas Nelson, 1981), p. 100.
7. Alli Worthington, *Breaking Busy.* (Grand Rapids, MI: Zondervan, 2016), pp. 142-143.
8. Jen Wilkin, ibid., p. 71.
9. Jerry Bridges, *Respectable Sins.* (Colorado Springs, CO: Navpress, 2007), p. 110.
10. Jerry Bridges, *Respectable Sins*, ibid., p. 111.
11. Jerry Bridges, *The Practice of Godliness*, ibid., pp. 164-165.

38477324R00056

Made in the USA
Middletown, DE
08 March 2019